I AM A Gun Safety ACTIVIST!

COLORING BOOK

Color your way into action!

c c r
p r e s s

Published by CCR Press
Austin, Texas
www.ccrpress.com

Copyright (C) 2020 by Casey Chapman Ross and CCR Press.

First published 2020

Manufactured in the United States

ISBN 978-1-7340503-2-5

Notice: The information in this book is true and complete to the best of our knowledge.
It is offered without guarantee on part of the author and publisher.
The author and publisher disclaim all liability in connection with the use of this book.

THANK YOU

I absolutely could not have accomplished this project without the
help of a talented and tireless team. Tiffany Harelik's project management knows no end, she is a warrior and
a great friend. Dylan Wickstrom's patience and persistence in taking my thoughts from concept to reality is
not taken for granted for a second. Zoe Kern's collaboration on the original I Am An Activist title made it all
feel possible and I will be forever grateful for her talent and inspiration.

Thank you to my kids for inspiring me to do more to help young people navigate the complicated waters of
gun safety and violence prevention in a way they can better understand. I love you all so much and will do any-
thing to help keep you safe.

Casey Chapman Ross

FOREWORD

"This book is important to use as a tool for young people who's voices have been left out of many conversations in the gun violence debate. Young people of color are disproportionately impacted by guns, and I hope this book will help us all re-imagine that another world is possible. I believe and know that another world is possible, one where we are not just talking about which individuals have access to guns, but one where people don't want to pick up guns in the first place."
--
Amber Goodwin
Executive Director
Community Justice Action Fund +
Community Justice Reform Coalition

"I Am A Gun Safety Activist! reassures our children by teaching them their voices matter - especially when it comes to feeling safe. An empowered child is a strong voice, pure in heart, free of fear and amplified for the greater good."
--
Ed Scruggs
Board President of Texas Gun Sense

Five years ago, I unknowingly put my three children in a potentially tragic situation. We attended a party at a friend's home, and didn't know that another guest had left his unlocked, loaded gun inside a backpack that was placed on the floor of the playroom. I remember noticing that backpack in the middle of the room; the kids played beside it, jumped over it, and pushed it out of their way. After the party, we were informed about the location of the loaded gun. I was shocked about how irresponsible the gun owner was, and furious at myself for having my kids in that environment. It's merely luck that none of the kids explored the contents of that backpack and that no tragedy occurred that day. We can't rely on luck. Each year, about 300 children access an unsecured firearm and unintentionally shoot themselves or someone else. These tragedies are preventable, and so are the gun suicides and homicides that occur after children access unsecured guns.

As adults, we need to always practice responsible gun storage: guns should be locked, unloaded and separate from ammunition. About 4.6 million kids in America live in homes with guns that are left unlocked and loaded. Because of this, we need to ask about responsible gun storage when our children visit other homes. This may seem like an awkward conversation, but it doesn't have to be. Remember, it's a conversation about safe gun storage, not about gun ownership. "How do you store any guns that you own?" is a simple, direct way to inquire about any unsecured firearms in order to determine if our children will be safe, just as we would discuss food allergies, pets, bike safety, etc. when visiting another home. As a volunteer who educates about responsible gun storage to prevent child gun access, I've seen how opening up this conversation in a non-judgemental way leads others to reassess their own gun storage methods and realize they should also be asking this question to others. I've had many gun safety discussions with my own children since that day five years ago. We talk about never touching a gun, never assuming it's a toy, and leaving the situation immediately and telling a trusted adult. However, they are still children and I can't fully rely on them when such serious consequences are at stake. Ultimately, safe gun storage is the responsibility of the adult gun owner, and as adults we can help spread the message of responsible gun storage within our own communities.
--
Jen Price
Lead Volunteer in the Effort to End Gun Violence

INTRO TO PARENTS

My goal for this book is to foster a healthy discussion around gun violence prevention between caretakers, educators and children. The activity of coloring is not only stress and anxiety reducing and good for brain health but provides a helpful distraction from the seriousness and pressure that sometimes comes with addressing big issues with children.

I highly encourage caretakers and children color alongside each other, as they discuss these big ideas and talk through the terms, actions, feelings and fears that may arise with each page. This book is meant to educate a young audience on gun safety and actions a young activist can take to begin familiaring them-selves with civic engagement and the movement to end gun violence. The Resources page in the back provides contact to valuable organizations for both getting involved, gun safety, keeping your home safe, suicide prevention and community programs available.

Always, always ASK if there is a gun in the home that your child is visiting. If there is, ask if it is locked away from the kids and if the ammo is kept in a separate place. Asking saves lives. *One in three homes contain at least one gun, with 265 million civilian-owned nationwide. It is our job as adults to keep our children safe from preventable gun violence/accidents.

*https://everytownresearch.org/secure-storage/

TABLE OF CONTENTS

I AM A GunSafety ACTIVIST!

COLORING BOOK

Color your way into action!

WHAT IS A GUN?

A METAL DEVICE THAT SENDS
METAL BULLETS THROUGH THE AIR VERY, VERY FAST.

WHAT SHOULD YOU DO IF YOU FIND ONE?

DON'T TOUCH IT. LEAVE THE ROOM & TELL AN ADULT RIGHT AWAY! YOU WILL NEVER BE IN TROUBLE FOR REPORTING A GUN. NEVER. YOUR SAFETY IS ALWAYS #1, ABOVE ALL ELSE.

COMMIT TO THE MISSION – EVERYONE DESERVES TO HAVE THEIR BODY BE SAFE.

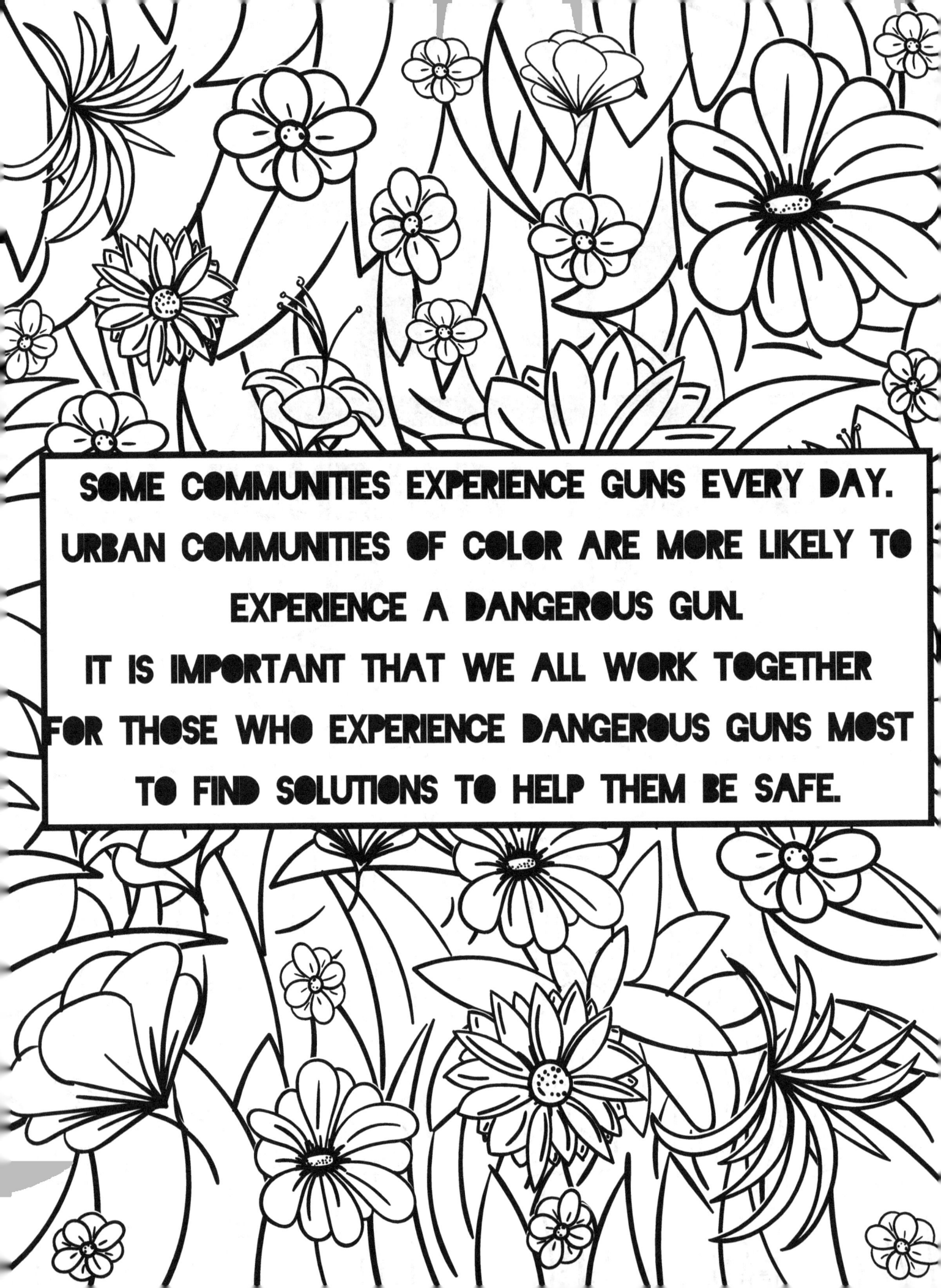

SOME COMMUNITIES EXPERIENCE GUNS EVERY DAY.
URBAN COMMUNITIES OF COLOR ARE MORE LIKELY TO
EXPERIENCE A DANGEROUS GUN.
IT IS IMPORTANT THAT WE ALL WORK TOGETHER
FOR THOSE WHO EXPERIENCE DANGEROUS GUNS MOST
TO FIND SOLUTIONS TO HELP THEM BE SAFE.

THE MORE WE GET TO KNOW OUR
FRIENDS AND NEIGHBORS, THE
BETTER WE CAN SUPPORT
ONE ANOTHER.

IF YOU SEE A FRIEND AT SCHOOL
THAT LOOKS LONELY, SAY HELLO.
MAKE FRIENDS WITH SOMEONE
THAT DOESN'T LOOK JUST LIKE YOU.
IT IS IMPORTANT WE LEARN FROM
ALL DIFFERENT KINDS OF FRIENDS.

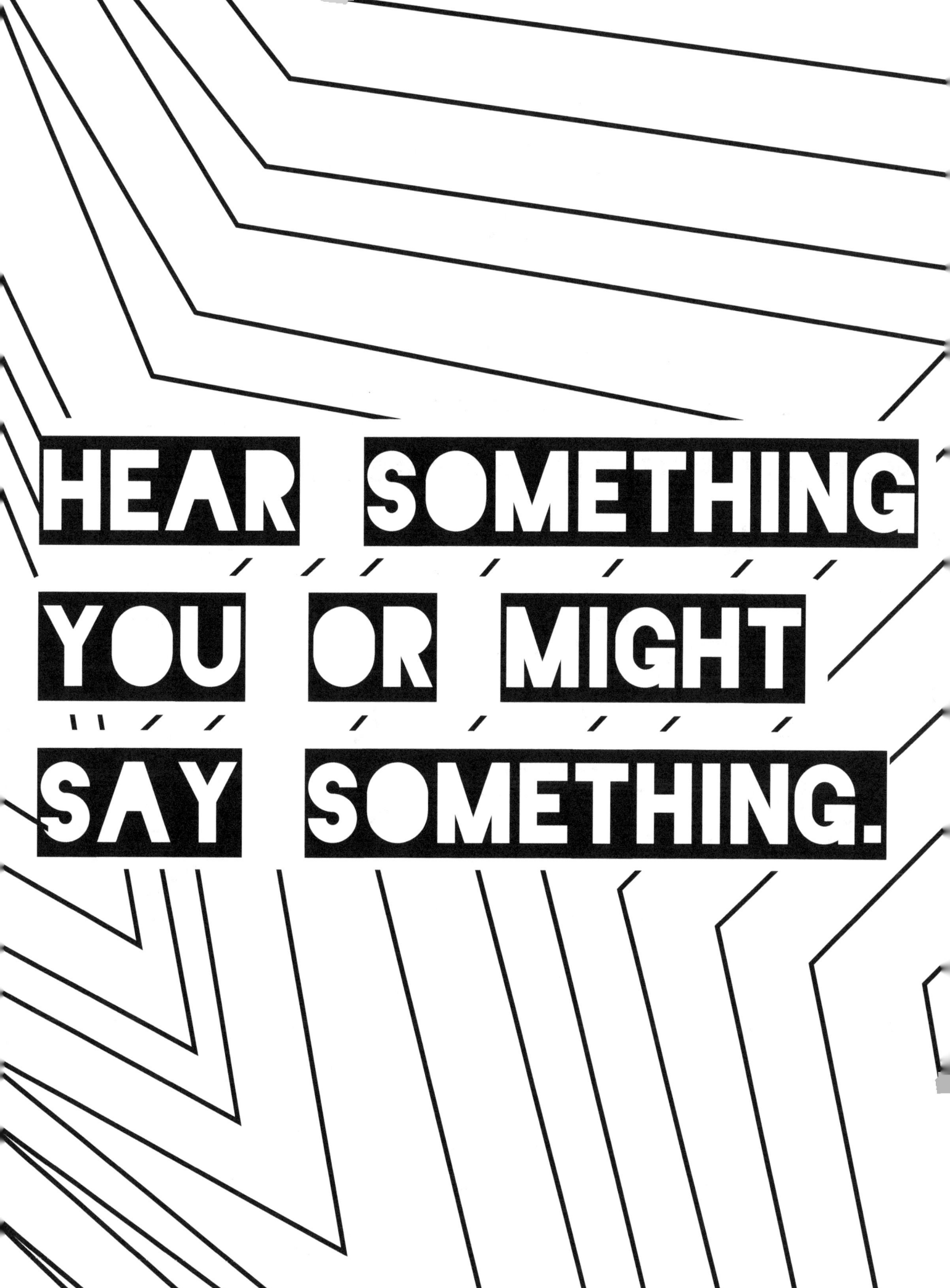

HERE ARE SOME THINGS THAT WILL HELP...

- UNIVERSAL BACKGROUND CHECKS
- WAITING PERIODS
- INVESTING IN COMMUNITY

PROGRAMS FOR HEALTHY AND SAFE KIDS

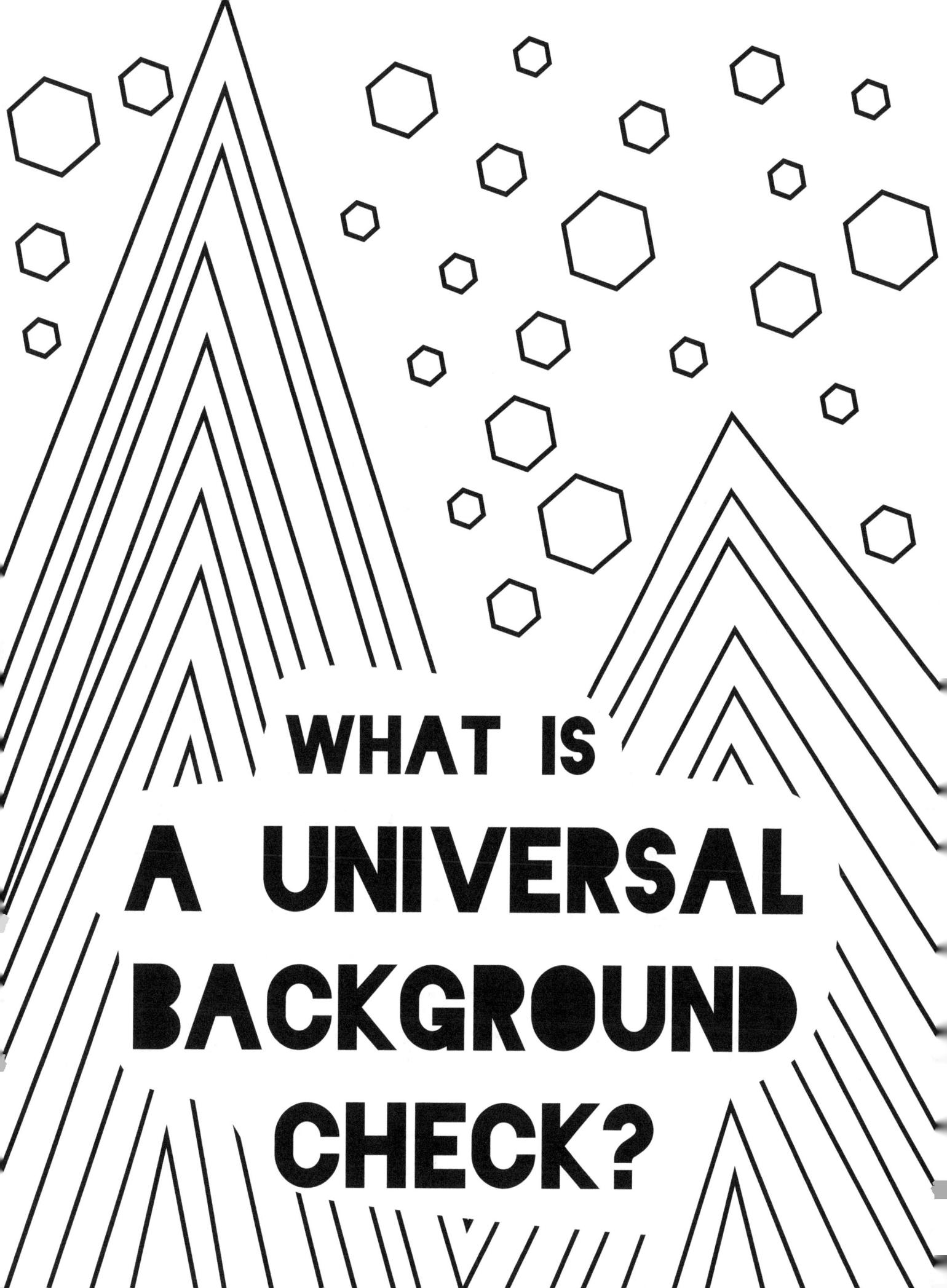

WHAT IS A UNIVERSAL BACKGROUND CHECK?

WHEN SOMEONE WANTS TO BUY A GUN, LAW ENFORCEMENT NEEDS TO CHECK FIRST TO SEE WHAT KINDS OF CHOICES THAT PERSON HAS MADE, HOW THEY HAVE USED TOOLS LIKE THIS BEFORE AND IF THEY FOLLOW THE LAW. MOST IMPORTANTLY, IT SHOULD APPLY TO ALL GUN SALES, NOT JUST SOME.

WHAT IS A WAITING PERIOD?

WHEN YOU DECIDE TO MAKE A BIG PURCHASE LIKE A GUN, IT'S A GOOD IDEA TO THINK ABOUT IT FIRST AND TO MAKE SURE YOU ARE READY FOR THE RESPONSIBILITY. IT'S IMPORTANT TO LEARN HOW TO USE IT SAFELY. IT'S ALSO IMPORTANT TO NOT BE IN A HURRY WHEN BUYING A GUN. A WAITING PERIOD IS A FEW DAYS BETWEEN WHEN SOMEONE BUYS A GUN AND WHEN THEY CAN USE IT.

WHAT CAN WE DO IN OUR COMMUNITIES?

BRINGING TOGETHER COMMUNITY OFFICIALS AND LEADERS WHO HAVE ESCAPED VIOLENCE TO HELP PEOPLE IN TROUBLE TO TURN THEIR LIVES AROUND.

O

INVESTING MONEY IN COMMUNITY PROGRAMS THAT ARE FOCUSED ON PUBLIC HEALTH.

O

ENCOURAGING HEALTH DEPARTMENTS, HOSPITALS, SCHOOLS, UNIVERSITIES, AND NON-PROFITS TO WORK TOGETHER TO FIND SOLUTIONS.

O

INCLUDING EVERYONE WHO HAS EXPERIENCE ON ALL SIDES OF THE GUN CRISIS IN DECISION-MAKING AND LAWS FOR THE FUTURE.

WHO ARE YOUR ELECTED OFFICIALS?

COLOR IN YOUR STATE ON THE MAP ABOVE!

My State is:_____.
My City is:_____.
My County is:_____.

VISIT:
ROCKTHEVOTE.com/action-center/

The President is:_____.
The Vice President is:_____.

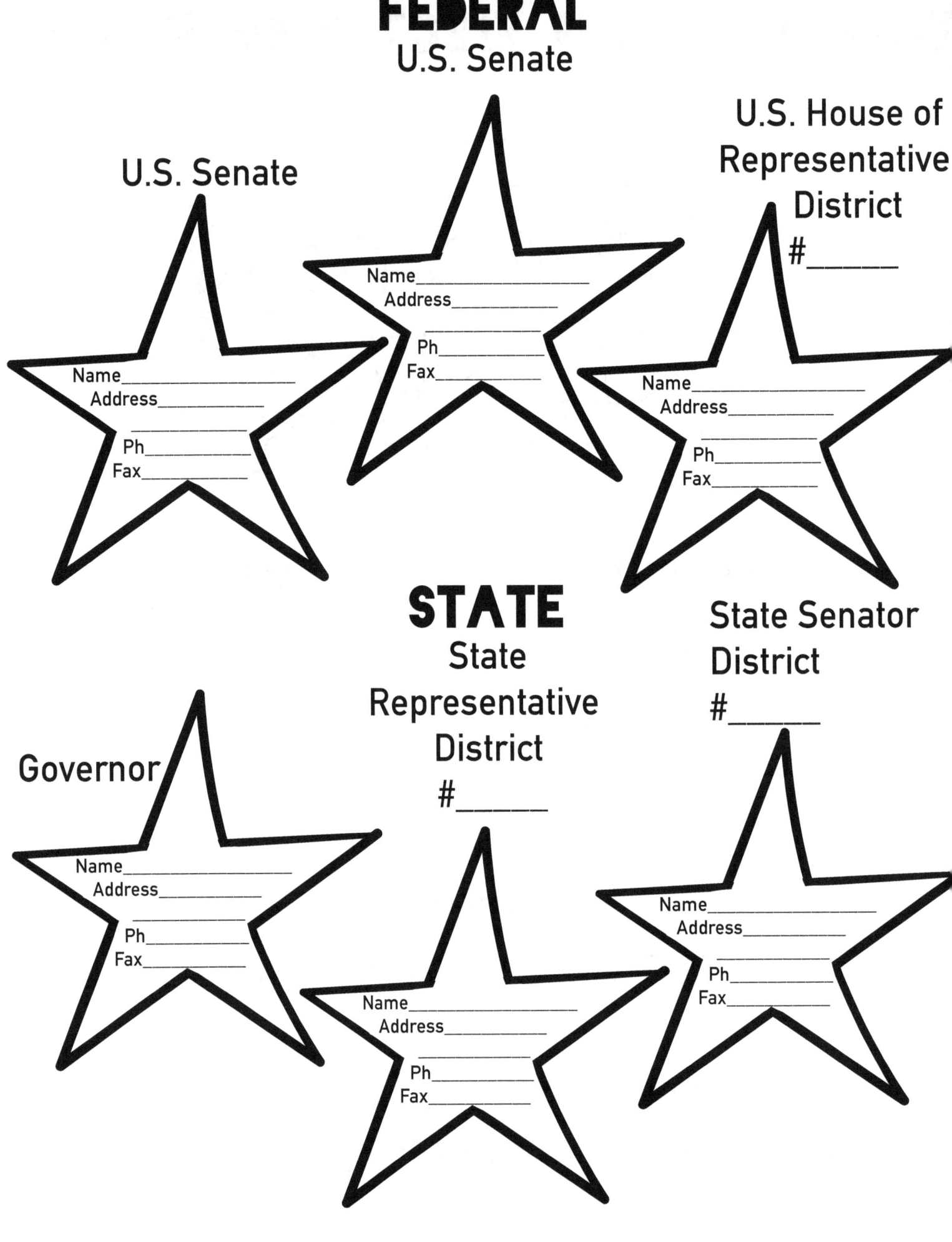

FEDERAL

U.S. Senate

U.S. Senate

U.S. House of Representative District #_____

Name_____
Address_____
_____
Ph_____
Fax_____

Name_____
Address_____
_____
Ph_____
Fax_____

Name_____
Address_____
_____
Ph_____
Fax_____

STATE

State Representative District #_____

State Senator District #_____

Governor

Name_____
Address_____
_____
Ph_____
Fax_____

Name_____
Address_____
_____
Ph_____
Fax_____

Name_____
Address_____
_____
Ph_____
Fax_____

WHAT DO I SAY?

CALL IN SCRIPT

"Hello, my name is _____ and I am a student at_____.

I am a member of the community you represent and support candidates that make gun safety a priority.

I appreciate you taking strong action in support of common sense gun reforms like universal background checks on all sales, waiting periods and community investments that support healthy and safe kids programming.

Thank you very much for your time. My address is

_____.

WHAT DO I WRITE?

WHAT ARE SOME LAWS YOU HAVE
LEARNED IN THIS BOOK THAT MIGHT MAKE
OUR COMMUNITY A SAFER PLACE?

FILL IN YOUR THOUGHTS ON THE LINES IN
THE LETTER.

BE POLITE AND TELL THEM WHAT YOU
CARE ABOUT AND WHY. PERSONAL LETTERS
BRIGHTEN PEOPLES DAY!

USE LOTS OF COLOR AND HAVE FUN
MAKING IT YOUR OWN!

1. FILL OUT 2. CUT OUT 3. FAX!
1. FILL OUT 2. CUT OUT 3. MAIL IN!

Did you know the #1 way to contact yourrepresentative is by fax?
It is rarely used anymore but every office has one,
so your message is sure to stand out!

I AM A
Gun Safety
ACTIVIST!

"Hello, my name is _____

and I am a student at _____.

I am a member of the community you represent and support candidates that make gun safety a priority. I appreciate you taking strong action in support of

1)_____

2)_____

3)_____

because_____

_____.

Thank you very much for your time.

Sincerely, a concerned citizen and future voter,

_____

My address is_____

_____

_____

www.ccrpress.com

1. FILL OUT 2. CUT OUT 3. FAX!
1. FILL OUT 2. CUT OUT 3. MAIL IN!

Did you know the #1 way to contact your representative is by fax?
It is rarely used anymore but every office has one,
so your message is sure to stand out!

I AM A
Gun Safety
ACTIVIST!

"Hello, my name is _____

and I am a student at _____.

I am a member of the community you represent and support candidates that make gun safety a priority. I appreciate you taking strong action in support of

1)_____

2)_____

3)_____

because_____

_____.

Thank you very much for your time.

Sincerely, a concerned citizen and future voter,

_____

My address is_____

_____

_____

1. FILL OUT 2. CUT OUT 3. FAX!
1. FILL OUT 2. CUT OUT 3. MAIL IN!

Did you know the #1 way to contact your representative is by fax?
It is rarely used anymore but every office has one,
so your message is sure to stand out!

I AM A
Gun Safety
ACTIVIST!

"Hello, my name is _____

and I am a student at _____.

I am a member of the community you represent and support candidates that make gun safety a priority. I appreciate you taking strong action in support of

1)_____

2)_____

3)_____

because_____

_____.

Thank you very much for your time.

Sincerely, a concerned citizen and future voter,

_____

My address is_____

_____

_____

www.ccrpress.com

1. FILL OUT 2. CUT OUT 3. FAX!
1. FILL OUT 2. CUT OUT 3. MAIL IN!

Did you know the #1 way to contact your representative is by fax?
It is rarely used anymore but every office has one,
so your message is sure to stand out!

I AM A
GunSafety
ACTIVIST!

"Hello, my name is _____

and I am a student at _____.

I am a member of the community you represent and support candidates that make gun safety a priority. I appreciate you taking strong action in support of

1)_____

2)_____

3)_____

because_____

_____.

Thank you very much for your time.

Sincerely, a concerned citizen and future voter,

_____

My address is_____

_____

_____

WHAT IS A MARCH?

A MARCH IS A GROUP OF PEOPLE WALKING TOGETHE
TO SEND A MESSAGE TO LEADERS.

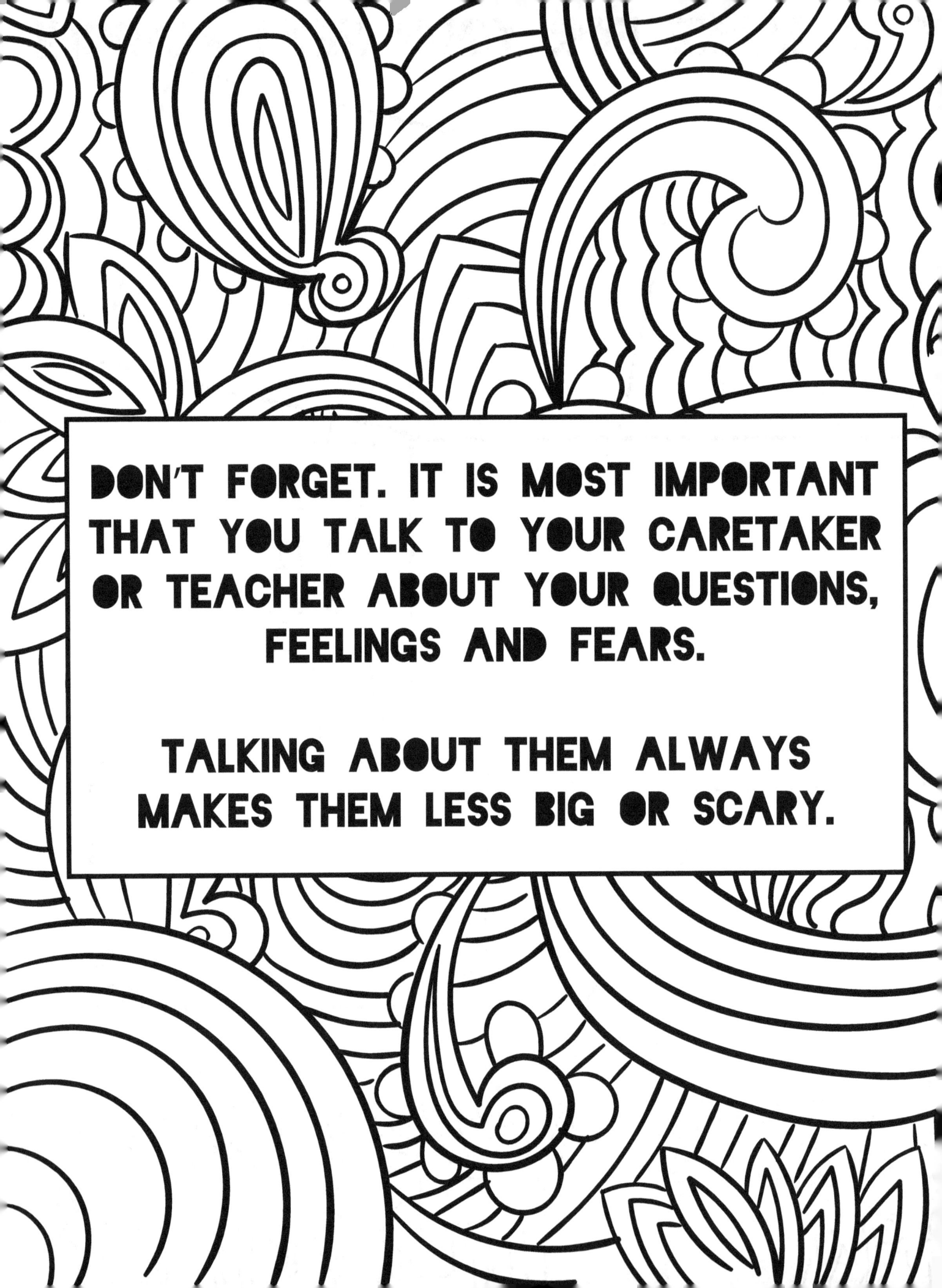

DON'T FORGET. IT IS MOST IMPORTANT THAT YOU TALK TO YOUR CARETAKER OR TEACHER ABOUT YOUR QUESTIONS, FEELINGS AND FEARS.

TALKING ABOUT THEM ALWAYS MAKES THEM LESS BIG OR SCARY.

HOW DO YOU FEEL?
(COLOR OR WRITE IN YOUR THOUGHTS.)

GLOSSARY

CITIZEN - someone who lives in a particular city, state, country

CONSTITUENT - a voting member of a commuity with the power to elect or appoint leader

CRIMINAL BACKGROUND CHECK SYSTEM (NICS)- to make sure the person buying a gun follows the law

GUN - a metal device that sends bullets through the air very, very fast

INCLUSION - making sure ALL people are respected and appreciated as valuable members of their communities.

INVESTING - spending time, energy and/or money toward something in hopes of a positive result

LAW - A law is a rule decided for the purpose of keeping the peace and security of society

MARCH - A group of people walking together to send a message to leaders in their community

PRESIDENT - The President of the United States (POTUS) is the head of the government of the United States of America and head of the Executive branch of government.

REPRESENTATIVE - a person chosen by an election or appointed to speak and make decisions on behalf of others in their community.

SENATOR - A senator is a person who works in the government. In the United States, senators are elected by voters to represent them in a state or federal senate. Each state elects two U.S. senators who serve six-year terms passing laws and voting on behalf of their communities.

THREE BRANCHES OF GOVERNMENT - Executive, Judicial and Legislative.

UNIVERSAL BACKGROUND CHECK - Requires all firearm sales be recorded and go through the National Instant Criminal Background Check System (NICS).

VICE PRESIDENT - The Vice President of the United States (POTUS) is just below the rank President of the United States and also part of the Executive Branch of government.

VIOLENCE - using physical force or power, verbally or physicallly against oneself, another person, or against a group or community, that causes harm or death.

WAITING PERIOD - period of time between when an action is requested and when it happens

WAITING PERIOD LAW - mandatory delay between the purchase and delivery of a gun which the gun owner must wait two to seven days before getting the gun.

RESOURCES

MARCH FOR OUR LIVES
https://marchforourlives.com/

EVERYTOWN
https://everytown.org/

MOMS DEMAND ACTION
https://momsdemandaction.org/

STUDENTS DEMAND ACTION
https://everytown.org/studentsdemand/

COMMUNITY JUSTICE ACTION FUND
https://www.cjactionfund.org

GUN SENSE VOTER
https://gunsensevoter.org/resources/

THE BRADY CAMPAIGN
https://www.bradyunited.org/

STATES UNITED TO PREVENT GUN VIOLENCE IN AMERICA
http://ceasefireusa.org/affiliates/

THE COALITION TO STOP GUN VIOLENCE
https://www.csgv.org/

GIFFORDS
https://giffords.org/

PREVENTION.ORG
https://www.preventioninstitute.org/

EDUCATIONAL FUND TO STOP GUN VIOLENCE
https://efsgv.org/

KIDS IN THE HOUSE
https://kids-clerk.house.gov

SANDY HOOK PROMISE
https://www.sandyhookpromise.org/

START WITH HELLO
https://www.sandyhookpromise.org/
startwithhello

ASK
https://www.bradyunited.org

BE SMART
http://besmartforkids.org/

TEXAS GUN SENSE
https://www.txgunsense.org/

NATIONAL SUICIDE PREVENTION HOTLINE
Call 1-800-273-8255
Available 24 hours everyday
https://suicidepreventionlifeline.org/
YOUTH: https://suicidepreventionlifeline.org/
help-yourself/youth/

YOU MATTER
https://youmatter.suicidepreventionlifeline.org

STOP BULLYING
https://www.stopbullying.gov/

HARVARD'S MEANS MATTER
https://www.hsph.harvard.edu/means-matter/

LOCK ARMS FOR LIFE
https://atcloserange.org/

PEACE IS A LIFESTYLE
https://www.peaceisalifestyle.com/beta/
lifecamp

Transparency/Disclosure: This coloring book is an original work by the author and is unrelated to any gun safety organization. Resources listed here were selected solely by the author to be provided as potential sites available to the public for further information on gun safety and violence prevention.

CHECK OUT THESE OTHER GREAT TITLES IN THE

COLORING BOOK SERIES:

I Am An Activist!

I Am A Gun Safety Activist!

I Am A Women's Rights Activist!

I Am An Immigration Reform Activist!

I Am A Climate Change Activist!

I Am A Health+care Activist!

I Am An Education Activist!

ABOUT THE AUTHOR:

Casey is an Austin native, graduated with a Fine Arts Degree in Studio Art from the University of Texas and has been a full-time freelance photographer for 7 years focusing on strengthening the efforts of the Democratic Party in Texas. In 2019, she opened CCR Press, a publishing label focusing on progressive titles. As a champion supporting the causes she holds dear, Casey is tireless in her efforts to lift up those causes with positive, powerful imagery.

ccr
press

www.ccrpress.com

CPSIA information can be obtained
at www.ICGtesting.com
Printed in the USA
LVHW061018090220
646310LV00019B/1523